Life Changing Quotes

for

Management,
Leadership
and
Work.

David Sparks

Contents

Introduction

Quotes seem to have a magical quality about them. For some reason, many people love reading them. Maybe its because the words speak to the person or maybe because they like and admire the author. Either way, quotes seem to carry an energy of their own, like a call to action.

Quotes can be inspirational to many, however just as many are not inspired. This may have to do with timing. When a reader reads a quote, they may not be in the appropriate state of mind, or the appropriate stage in their life to appreciate the meaning or lessons behind the words.

As a teacher I have displayed quite a few quotes around my classroom with the hope that one of them will inspire the students and motivate them to work that little bit harder. I was truly amazed when I received a phone call from parents of a student, thanking me for what I had said in class one day. These parents had been having difficulty with their 15-year-old son for quite some time, but he did a turn around after reading one of the new quotes I had put up in the room. The quote was **"time is all you've got and time is running out."** I had heard it while listening to a Jim Rohn tape and thought it would be useful to the students, as school would finish before they knew it.

The quotes written in this book are specifically about Management, Leadership and Work. These are three very important areas of life, which contribute to our wellbeing, and sense of accomplishment. When we work we are either part of management or part of the leadership team of the organization in which we work, or our work is influenced and directed by managers and/or leaders.

Sometimes we think that we are being led by incompetents, but we fail to realise or are not aware of the complexity of what they are expected to do. It is easy for employees to criticise when they don't have the whole picture, which is in itself a problem. Management should probably include the employees in some decision-making as many employees could be skilled in areas management and leadership may not be aware of. Employees who are consulted tend to put more effort into their work, especially when they see their ideas being implemented. But of course management and leaders already know this.

On the other side of it, if employees put more effort into their work and treated the organization as if it were their own, they would be recognized for increased productivity and most likely be promoted on their merit. Unfortunately however, many employees don't see the contribution they are making, instead they see themselves in a job which they must endure.

The words in this book come from actors and actresses, athletes, businessmen and women, politicians, musicians, philosophers, scientists and more. Some quotes go back as far as ancient Rome and ancient Greece and are still relevant to this day.

I suggest this book be used as a regular 'go to', so keep it handy and look at it often. You may read something now which may not resonate with you at this point in your life, but a year or two down the track, it will have a totally different meaning.

You will notice that a few quotes sound the same, but come from different authors. I have put this down to the individuals being on the same wavelength and their experiences having led them to formulate similar beliefs.

Of course, you probably won't find every quote useful or inspiring, but this is to be expected. Since everyone's values are different, different quotations will inspire different people.

Hopefully you will enjoy these quotes for a long time to come and notice the improvements that benefit your life by making the small changes that these sages provoke.

Management

Management is nothing more than motivating other people.

- Lee Iacocca

Management is efficiency in climbing the ladder of success; leadership determines whether the ladder is leaning against the right wall.

- Stephen Covey

Success in management requires learning as fast as the world is changing.

- Warren Bennis

A smart manager will establish a culture of gratitude. Expand the appreciative attitude to suppliers, vendors, delivery people, and of course, customers.

- Harvey Mackay

A manager is responsible for the application and performance of knowledge.

- Peter Drucker

Managers in all too many American companies do not achieve the desired results because nobody makes them do it.

- Harold S. Geneen

Good management is the art of making problems so interesting and their solutions so constructive that everyone wants to get to work and deal with them.

- Paul Hawken

A manager is not a person who can do the work better than his men; he is a person who can get his men to do the work better than he can.

- Frederick W. Smith

Most of what we call management consists of making it difficult for people to get their work done.

- Peter Drucker

If you hire people just because they can do a job, they'll work for your money. But if you hire people who believe what you believe, they'll work for you with blood, sweat, and tears.

- Simon Sinek

It's not the tools that you have faith in - tools are just tools. They work, or they don't work. It's people you have faith in or not. Yeah, sure, I'm still optimistic I mean, I get pessimistic sometimes but not for long.

- Steve Jobs

Management is doing things right; leadership is doing the right things.

- Peter Drucker

Employees who believe that management is concerned about them as a whole person - not just an employee - are more productive, more satisfied, more fulfilled. Satisfied employees mean satisfied customers, which leads to profitability.

- Anne M. Mulcahy

Effective leadership is putting first things first. Effective management is discipline, carrying it out.

- Stephen Covey

Management is about arranging and telling. Leadership is about nurturing and enhancing.

- Tom Peters

Leadership is working with goals and vision; management is working with objectives.

- Russel Honore

Management by objective works - if you know the objectives. Ninety percent of the time you don't.

- Peter Drucker

Management is all about managing in the short term, while developing the plans for the long term.

- Jack Welch

The first rule of management is delegation. Don't try and do everything yourself because you can't.

- Anthea Turner

Many think of management as cutting deals and laying people off and hiring people and buying and selling companies. That's not management, that's deal making. Management is the opportunity to help people become better people. Practiced that way, it's a magnificent profession.

- Clayton M. Christensen

The art of effective listening is essential to clear communication, and clear communication is necessary to management success.

- James Cash Penney

Practice Golden-Rule 1 of Management in everything you do. Manage others the way you would like to be managed.

- Brian Tracy

Success in management requires learning as fast as the world is changing.

- Warren Bennis

No nation has embraced Total Quality Management, e-commerce and e-government with greater enthusiasm than Dubai. Such innovations have given Dubai a competitive edge and an accelerated growth rate that few could match.

- Abdul Aziz Al Ghurair

Most of what we call management consists of making it difficult for people to get their work done.

- Peter Drucker

Good management consists in showing average people how to do the work of superior people.

- John D. Rockefeller

The way management treats associates is exactly how the associates will treat the customers.

- Sam Walton

The fish stinks from the head down

- Unknown

Divorced from ethics, leadership is reduced to management and politics to mere technique.

- James MacGregor Burns

Effective management always means asking the right question.

- Robert Heller

I think that the best training a top manager can be engaged in is management by example.

- Carlos Ghosn

The secret to winning is constant, consistent management.

- Tom Landry

Management must speak with one voice. When it doesn't management itself becomes a peripheral opponent to the team's mission.

- Pat Riley

The key to management is to get rid of the managers.

- Ricardo Semler

You can teach all sorts of things that improve the practice of management with people who are managers. What you cannot do is teach management to somebody who is not a manager, the way you cannot teach surgery to somebody whose not a surgeon.

- Henry Mintzberg

When I got to GM they were using a matrix method of management which means everybody has more than one boss. I first heard about that system many years ago. It's supposed to help with collaboration, but my assessment is that it's pretty hard to get geared for action that way.

- Edward Whitacre, Jr.

Because management deals mostly with the status quo and leadership deals mostly with change, in the next century we are going to have to try to become much more skilled at creating leaders.

- John P. Kotter

What should be the aim of management? What is their job? Quality is the responsibility of the top people. Its origin is in the boardroom. They are the ones who decide.

- W. Edwards Deming

The first myth of management is that it exists. The second myth of management is that success equals skill.

- Robert Heller

Corporate culture matters. How management chooses to treat its people impacts everything - for better or for worse.

- Simon Sinek

When you think of all the conflicts we have - whether those conflicts are local, whether they are regional or global - these conflicts are often over the management, the distribution of resources. If these resources are very valuable, if these resources are scarce, if these resources are degraded, there is going to be competition.

- Wangari Maathai

All businesses require capital, management and labor, and business executives, wanting to grow and maintain profitable enterprises, have a strong incentive to keep costs, including labor, as low as possible.

- Kevin O'Leary

Lots of folks confuse bad management with destiny.

- Kin Hubbard

Eliminate numerical quotas, including Management by Objectives.

- W. Edwards Deming

Reduce the layers of management. They put distance between the top of an organization and the customers.

- Donald Rumsfeld

The kind of people I look for to fill top management spots are the eager beavers, the mavericks. These are the guys who try to do more than they're expected to do - they always reach.

- Lee Iacocca

Bosses should sanction the nap rather than expect workers to power on all day without repose. They might even find that workers' happiness - or what management types refer to as 'employee satisfaction results' - might improve.

- Tom Hodgkinson

Specialized management courses are useful but should come well after the complexity of management and business are understood.

- Warren Bennis

We're not in an information age anymore. We're in the information management age.

- Chris Hardwick

Being a consultant is like flying first-class. The food is terrific, the drinks are cold. But all you can do is walk up to the pilot and say, 'bank left.' If you're in management, you have the controls.

- Greg Brenneman

You read these management books that say, 'These are the hard things about running a company.' But those aren't really the hard things. The hard things are when you have to layoff half your company, or you have to fire your best friend. Or you have to figure out a way not to go bankrupt.

- Ben Horowitz

You can be stern and forthright, and that's my management style, but when you lose it totally, that's a sign of weakness.

- Jon Huntsman, Jr.

But charity is a very complicated thing. It's important to find an area where you can really help and you can feel the results. Charity is not like feeding pigeons in the square. It is a process that requires professional management.

- Roman Abramovich

We all know business financial performance improves when more women are in senior levels of management and leadership.

- Beth Brooke

Management's job is to convey leadership's message in a compelling and inspiring way. Not just in meetings, but also by example.

- Jeffrey Gitomer

Reading a book about management isn't going to make you a good manager any more than a book about guitar will make you a good guitarist, but it can get you thinking about the most important concepts.

- Drew Houston

The prevailing system of management has crushed fun out of the workplace.

- W. Edwards Deming

Investing in management means building communication systems, business processes, feedback, and routines that let you scale the business and team as efficiently as possible.

- Fred Wilson

It is not enough to have great qualities; we should also have the management of them.

- Francois de La Rochefoucauld

Management must manage!

- Harold S. Geneen

Export anything to a friendly country except American management.

- W. Edwards Deming

The biggest barriers to strategic renewal are almost always top management's unexamined beliefs.

- Gary Hamel

Management manages by making decisions and by seeing that those decisions are implemented.

- Harold S. Geneen

Management innovation is going to be the most enduring source of competitive advantage. There will be lots of rewards for firms in the vanguard.

- Gary Hamel

When I finally got a management position, I found out how hard it is to lead and manage people.

- Guy Kawasaki

Management is the opportunity to help people become better people. Practiced that way, it's a magnificent profession.

- Clayton Christensen

The key to being a good manager is keeping the people who hate me away from those who are still undecided.

- Casey Stengel

Employees will do to the organization the same as what management does to the employees.

- Robert Jamgotchian

<u>Leadership</u>

True leadership lies in guiding others to success. In ensuring that everyone is performing at their best, doing the work they are pledged to do and doing it well.

- Bill Owens

It will be disastrous when a leader or manager shows up with one attitude one day and treats people with a different attitude the next day.

- Zig Ziglar

A leader is best when people barely know he exists, when his work is done, his aim fulfilled, they will say: we did it ourselves.

- Lao Tzu

Teamwork makes the dream work, but a vision becomes a nightmare when the leader has a big dream and a bad team.

- John C. Maxwell

A gentle word, a kind look, a good-natured smile can work wonders and accomplish miracles.

- William Hazlitt

Leadership is not about a title or a designation. It's about impact, influence and inspiration. Impact involves getting results, influence is about spreading the passion you have for your work, and you have to inspire team-mates and customers.

- Robin S. Sharma

Leaders aren't born they are made. And they are made just like anything else, through hard work. And that's the price we'll have to pay to achieve that goal, or any goal.

- Vince Lombardi

Let me define a leader. He must have vision and passion and not be afraid of any problem. Instead, he should know how to defeat it. Most importantly, he must work with integrity.

- A. P. J. Abdul Kalam

I know of no single formula for success. But over the years I have observed that some attributes of leadership are universal and are often about finding ways of encouraging people to combine their efforts, their talents, their insights, their enthusiasm and their inspiration to work together.

- Queen Elizabeth II

If you want to build a ship, don't drum up people to collect wood and don't assign them tasks and work, but rather teach them to long for the endless immensity of the sea.

- Antoine de Saint-Exupery

A leader's job is not to do the work for others, it's to help others figure out how to do it themselves, to get things done, and to succeed beyond what they thought possible.

- Simon Sinek

A good boss makes his men realize they have more ability than they think they have so that they consistently do better work than they thought they could.

- Charles Erwin Wilson

Good leadership consists of showing average people how to do the work of superior people.

- John D. Rockefeller

When the best leader's work is done the people say, 'We did it ourselves.'

- Lao Tzu

Leadership is a mindset that shifts from being a victim to creating results. Any one of us can demonstrate leadership in our work and within our lives.

- Robin S. Sharma

Trust is the lubrication that makes it possible for organizations to work.

- Warren Bennis

Your most precious possession is not your financial assets. Your most precious possession is the people you have working there, and what they carry around in their heads, and their ability to work together.

- Robert Reich

If your actions inspire others to dream more, learn more, do more and become more, you are a leader.

- John Quincy Adams

A leader is one who knows the way, goes the way, and shows the way.

- John C. Maxwell

It is better to lead from behind and to put others in front, especially when you celebrate victory when nice things occur. You take the front line when there is danger. Then people will appreciate your leadership.

- Nelson Mandela

A good leader takes a little more than his share of the blame, a little less than his share of the credit.

- Arnold H. Glasow

Leadership and learning are indispensable to each other.

- John F. Kennedy

Don't find fault, find a remedy.

- Henry Ford

Leadership is solving problems. The day soldiers stop bringing you their problems is the day you have stopped leading them. They have either lost confidence that you can help or concluded you do not care. Either case is a failure of leadership.

- Colin Powell

Be a yardstick of quality. Some people aren't used to an environment where excellence is expected.

- Steve Jobs

A leader is best when people barely know he exists, when his work is done, his aim fulfilled, they will say: we did it ourselves.

- Lao Tzu

Outstanding leaders go out of their way to boost the self-esteem of their personnel. If people believe in themselves, it's amazing what they can accomplish.

- Sam Walton

A genuine leader is not a searcher for consensus but a molder of consensus.

- Martin Luther King, Jr.

The quality of a leader is reflected in the standards they set for themselves.

- Ray Kroc

People ask the difference between a leader and a boss. The leader leads, and the boss drives.

- Theodore Roosevelt

Leadership - leadership is about taking responsibility, not making excuses.

- Mitt Romney

Leadership is the capacity to translate vision into reality.

- Warren Bennis

I suppose leadership at one time meant muscles; but today it means getting along with people.

- Mahatma Gandhi

When your values are clear to you, making decisions becomes easier.

- Roy E. Disney

The task of the leader is to get his people from where they are to where they have not been.

- Henry A. Kissinger

High expectations are the key to everything.

- Sam Walton

Effective leadership is not about making speeches or being liked; leadership is defined by results not attributes.

- Peter Drucker

Leadership cannot really be taught. It can only be learned.

- Harold S. Geneen

Only the guy who isn't rowing has time to rock the boat.

- Jean-Paul Sartre

Go as far as you can see; when you get there, you'll be able to see farther.

- J. P. Morgan

No man will make a great leader who wants to do it all himself or get all the credit for doing it.

- Andrew Carnegie

Leadership is unlocking people's potential to become better.

- Bill Bradley

Leadership is the art of getting someone else to do something you want done because he wants to do it.

- Dwight D. Eisenhower

A leader is a dealer in hope.

- Napoleon Bonaparte

Leaders must be close enough to relate to others, but far enough ahead to motivate them.

- John C. Maxwell

Management is about arranging and telling. Leadership is about nurturing and enhancing.

- Tom Peters

It is better to have a lion at the head of an army of sheep, than a sheep at the head of an army of lions.

- Daniel Defoe

Be careful the environment you choose for it will shape you; be careful the friends you choose for you will become like them.

- W. Clement Stone

People who enjoy meetings should not be in charge of anything.

- Thomas Sowell

A man who wants to lead the orchestra must turn his back on the crowd.

- Max Lucado

Think little goals and expect little achievements. Think big goals and win big success.

- David Joseph Schwartz

Hold yourself responsible for a higher standard than anybody expects of you. Never excuse yourself.

- Henry Ward Beecher

Good leadership consists of showing average people how to do the work of superior people.

- John D. Rockefeller

The art of leadership is saying no, not saying yes. It is very easy to say yes.

- Tony Blair

Without initiative, leaders are simply workers in leadership positions.

> — Bo Bennett

People buy into the leader before they buy into the vision.

> — John C. Maxwell

If a window of opportunity appears, don't pull down the shade.

> — Tom Peters

I don't know any other way to lead but by example.

> — Don Shula

Leadership consists of picking good men and helping them do their best.

> — Chester W. Nimitz

Leadership is practiced not so much in words as in attitude and in actions.

> — Harold S. Geneen

Today a reader, tomorrow a leader.

> — Margaret Fuller

Lead, follow, or get out of the way.

- Laurence J. Peter

A leader does not deserve the name unless he is willing occasionally to stand alone.

- Henry A. Kissinger

Leaders must encourage their organizations to dance to forms of music yet to be heard.

- Warren Bennis

Be the chief but never the lord.

- Lao Tzu

You're only as good as the people you hire.

- Ray Kroc

Great companies in the way they work, start with great leaders.

- Steve Ballmer

Time is neutral and does not change things. With courage and initiative, leaders change things.

- Jesse Jackson

When placed in command, take charge.

- Norman Schwarzkopf

The real leader has no need to lead - he is content to point the way.

- Henry Miller

The employer generally gets the employees he deserves.

- J. Paul Getty

If you command wisely, you'll be obeyed cheerfully.

- Thomas Fuller

You have to lead people gently toward what they already know is right.

- Phil Crosby

One must be convinced to convince, to have enthusiasm to stimulate the others.

- Stefan Zweig

What helps people helps business.

- Leo Burnett

The very exercise of leadership fosters capacity for it.

- Cyril Falls

The supreme quality for leadership is unquestionably integrity. Without it, no real success is possible, no matter whether it is on a section gang, a football field, in an army, or in an office.

- Dwight D. Eisenhower

No matter how good you think you are as a leader, my goodness, the people around you will have all kinds of ideas for how you can get better. So for me, the most fundamental thing about leadership is to have the humility to continue to get feedback and to try to get better - because your job is to try to help everybody else get better.

- Jim Yong Kim

Leadership is not about a title or a designation. It's about impact, influence and inspiration. Impact involves getting results, influence is about spreading the passion you have for your work, and you have to inspire team-mates and customers.

- Robin S. Sharma

The growth and development of people is the highest calling of leadership.

- Harvey S. Firestone

Ultimately, leadership is not about glorious crowning acts. It's about keeping your team focused on a goal and motivated to do their best to achieve it, especially when the stakes are high and the consequences really matter. It is about laying the groundwork for others' success, and then standing back and letting them shine.

- Chris Hadfield

Men make history and not the other way around. In periods where there is no leadership, society stands still. Progress occurs when courageous, skilful leaders seize the opportunity to change things for the better.

- Harry S Truman

Leadership is not about the next election; it's about the next generation.

- Simon Sinek

Most businesses think that product is the most important thing, but without great leadership, mission and a team that deliver results at a high level, even the best product won't make a company successful.

- Robert Kiyosaki

One of the tests of leadership is the ability to recognize a problem before it becomes an emergency.

- Arnold H. Glasow

Leadership is not a popularity contest; it's about leaving your ego at the door. The name of the game is to lead without a title.

- Robin S. Sharma

Leadership is working with goals and vision; management is working with objectives.

- Russel Honore

I think one of the keys to leadership is recognizing that everybody has gifts and talents. A good leader will learn how to harness those gifts toward the same goal.

- Benjamin Carson

There are good leaders who actively guide and bad leaders who actively misguide. Hence, leadership is about persuasion, presentation and people skills.

- Shiv Khera

The test of leadership is not to put greatness into humanity, but to elicit it, for the greatness is already there.

- James Buchanan

Leadership is a potent combination of strategy and character. But if you must be without one, be without the strategy.

- **Norman Schwarzkopf**

A good objective of leadership is to help those who are doing poorly to do well and to help those who are doing well to do even better.

- **Jim Rohn**

Leadership is hard to define and good leadership even harder. But if you can get people to follow you to the ends of the earth, you are a great leader.

- **Indra Nooyi**

You learn far more from negative leadership than from positive leadership. Because you learn how not to do it. And, therefore, you learn how to do it.

- **Norman Schwarzkopf**

Leadership is getting someone to do what they don't want to do, to achieve what they want to achieve.

- **Tom Landry**

One of the best paradoxes of leadership is a leader's need to be both stubborn and open-minded. A leader must insist on sticking to the vision and stay on course to the destination. But he must be open-minded during the process.

- Simon Sinek

The function of leadership is to produce more leaders, not more followers.

- Ralph Nader

The secret to success is good leadership, and good leadership is all about making the lives of your team members or workers better.

- Tony Dungy

I wish I had played team sports. I think every kid should. Teamwork builds character - teaches people about leadership and cooperation.

- Mo Rocca

Leadership is a way of thinking, a way of acting and, most importantly, a way of communicating.

- Simon Sinek

To me, leadership is about encouraging people. It's about stimulating them. It's about enabling them to achieve what they can achieve - and to do that with a purpose.

- Christine Lagarde

Leadership is about vision and responsibility, not power.

- Seth Berkley

Lead yourself whenever your boss' leadership deteriorates. When your boss doesn't praise what you do, praise yourself. When your boss doesn't make you big, make yourself big. Remember, if you have done your best, failure does not count.

- Mario Teguh

A leadership culture is one where everyone thinks like an owner, a CEO or a managing director. It's one where everyone is entrepreneurial and proactive.

- Robin S. Sharma

No institution can possibly survive if it needs geniuses or supermen to manage it. It must be organized in such a way as to be able to get along under a leadership composed of average human beings.

- Peter Drucker

Leadership is a mindset that shifts from being a victim to creating results. Any one of us can demonstrate leadership in our work and within our lives.

- Robin S. Sharma

Leadership is a choice, not a position.

- Stephen Covey

You have to enable and empower people to make decisions independent of you. As I've learned, each person on a team is an extension of your leadership; if they feel empowered by you they will magnify your power to lead.

- Tom Ridge

True leadership lies in guiding others to success. In ensuring that everyone is performing at their best, doing the work they are pledged to do and doing it well.

- Bill Owens

If there is such a thing as good leadership, it is to give a good example. I have to do so for all the Ikea employees.

- Ingvar Kamprad

Character matters; leadership descends from character.

- Rush Limbaugh

You don't lead by hitting people over the head - that's assault, not leadership.

- **Dwight D. Eisenhower**

Inability to make decisions is one of the principal reasons executives fail. Deficiency in decision-making ranks much higher than lack of specific knowledge or technical know-how as an indicator of leadership failure.

- **John C. Maxwell**

Leadership is a matter of having people look at you and gain confidence, seeing how you react. If you're in control, they're in control.

- **Tom Landry**

The signs of outstanding leadership appear primarily among the followers. Are the followers reaching their potential? Are they learning? Serving? Do they achieve the required results? Do they change with grace? Manage conflict?

- **Max de Pree**

Leadership is simply the ability of an individual to coalesce the efforts of other individuals toward achieving common goals. It boils down to looking after your people and ensuring that, from top to bottom, everyone feels part of the team.

- Frederick W. Smith

Inspirational leaders need to have a winning mentality in order to inspire respect. It is hard to trust in the leadership of someone who is half-hearted about their purpose, or only sporadic in focus or enthusiasm.

- Sebastian Coe

Leadership is all about taking people on a journey. The challenge is that most of the time, we are asking people to follow us to places we ourselves have never been.

- Andy Stanley

It is the responsibility of leadership to provide opportunity, and the responsibility of individuals to contribute.

- William Pollard

Leadership has a harder job to do than just choose sides. It must bring sides together.

- Jesse Jackson

Real leadership is leaders recognizing that they serve the people that they lead.

- Pete Hoekstra

Anyone can show exceptional leadership ability in easy times. When all's going to plan, anyone can be inspirational/excellent/innovative and strong. The real question is how do you show up when everything's falling apart?

- Robin S. Sharma

A leader is one who, out of madness or goodness, volunteers to take upon himself the woe of the people. There are few men so foolish, hence the erratic quality of leadership in the world.

- John Updike

The key to successful leadership today is influence, not authority.

- Ken Blanchard

Leadership is a privilege to better the lives of others. It is not an opportunity to satisfy personal greed.

- Mwai Kibaki

The art of communication is the language of leadership.

- James Humes

Leadership is about being a servant first.

- Allen West

Leadership offers an opportunity to make a difference in someone's life, no matter what the project.

- Bill Owens

Leadership comes in small acts as well as bold strokes.

- Carly Fiorina

The role of leadership is to transform the complex situation into small pieces and prioritize them.

- Carlos Ghosn

I think leadership is service and there is power in that giving: to help people, to inspire and motivate them to reach their fullest potential.

- Denise Morrison

Leadership consists not in degrees of technique but in traits of character; it requires moral rather than athletic or intellectual effort, and it imposes on both leader and follower alike the burdens of self-restraint.

- Lewis H. Lapham

The cost of leadership is self-interest.

- Simon Sinek

One of the most important things about leadership is that you have to have the kind of humility that will allow you to be coached.

- Jim Yong Kim

Leadership is about doing what you know is right - even when a growing din of voices around you is trying to convince you to accept what you know to be wrong.

- Bob Ehrlich

Leadership demands that we make tough choices.

- Alan Autry

I think that in any group activity - whether it be business, sports, or family - there has to be leadership or it won't be successful.

- **John Wooden**

I have a different vision of leadership. A leadership is someone who brings people together.

- **George W. Bush**

At the end the day because I believe so strongly in leadership, what I look for first, what I try to assess, is integrity.

- **Kenneth Chenault**

If you don't understand that you work for your mislabelled 'subordinates', then you know nothing of leadership. You know only tyranny.

- **Dee Hock**

Humility is a great quality of leadership which derives respect and not just fear or hatred.

- **Yousef Munayyer**

My best investment, as clichéd as this sounds, is the money I've spent developing myself, via books, workshops and coaching. Leadership begins within, and to have a better career, start by building a better you.

- Robin S. Sharma

Most leadership strategies are doomed to failure from the outset. As people have been noting for years, the majority of strategic initiatives that are driven from the top are marginally effective - at best.

- Peter Senge

Leadership is an opportunity to serve. It is not a trumpet call to self-importance.

- J. Donald Walters

There are very few good examples of effective, nurturing leadership that unlocks people's potential or even enthusiasm.

- Deepak Chopra

I forgot to shake hands and be friendly. It was an important lesson about leadership.

- Lee Iacocca

Character matters; leadership descends from character.

- Rush Limbaugh

The world is starving for original and decisive leadership.

- Bryant H. McGill

Humility is a great quality of leadership which derives respect and not just fear or hatred.

- Yousef Munayyer

Don't necessarily avoid sharp edges. Occasionally they are necessary to leadership.

- Donald Rumsfeld

Pay attention to those employees who respectfully ask why. They are demonstrating an interest in their jobs and exhibiting a curiosity that could eventually translate into leadership ability.

- Harvey Mackay

Leadership is, among other things, the ability to inflict pain and get away with it - short-term pain for long-term gain.

- George Will

Leadership means forming a team and working toward common objectives that are tied to time, metrics, and resources.

- Russel Honore

Leadership requires the courage to make decisions that will benefit the next generation.

- Alan Autry

Uncertainty is a permanent part of the leadership landscape. It never goes away.

- Andy Stanley

Turnaround or growth, it's getting your people focused on the goal that is still the job of leadership.

- Anne M. Mulcahy

What I've really learned over time is that optimism is a very, very important part of leadership.

- Bob Iger

Leadership appears to be the art of getting others to want to do something you are convinced should be done.

- Vance Packard

Not everybody is created equal, and it's important for companies to identify those high potentials and treat them differently, accelerate their development and pay them more. That process is so incredibly important to developing first-class leadership in a company.

- Anne M. Mulcahy

Well, I think that - I think leadership's always been about two main things: imagination and courage.

- Paul Keating

I think we need leadership that helps us remember that part of what we are about is caring about more than the person right next to us, but the folks across the way.

- Anna Deavere Smith

Real leadership means tackling tough problems ourselves and not leaving them to our children.

- Jon Kyl

My four years in the Marine Corps left me with an indelible understanding of the value of leadership skills.

- Frederick W. Smith

I think we so often equate leadership with being experts - the leader is supposed to come in and fix things. But in this interconnected world we live in now, it's almost impossible for just one person to do that.

- Jacqueline Novogratz

Actions, not words, are the ultimate results of leadership.

- Bill Owens

There is no greater name for a leader than mother or father. There is no leadership more important than parenthood.

- Sheri L. Dew

One of the lessons of leadership worth emphasizing is that you want to get to know other great leaders and take their advice. At some point in your development, it's only people who've been in the seat of having to be leaders who can help you in a deep way.

- Jim Yong Kim

Leadership is particularly necessary to ensure ready acceptance of the unfamiliar and that which is contrary to tradition.

- Cyril Falls

Different times need different types of leadership.

- Park Geun-hye

Management's job is to convey leadership's message in a compelling and inspiring way. Not just in meetings, but also by example.

- Jeffrey Gitomer

A big part of leadership is just being comfortable with the fact that some decisions really are only yours.

- Helene D. Gayle

Absolute identity with one's cause is the first and great condition of successful leadership.

- Woodrow Wilson

We in the press, by our power, can actually undermine leadership.

- Christiane Amanpour

Leadership - mobilization toward a common goal.

- Garry Wills

A good part of my leadership skills is crafted from learning from experiences early in my career that were not positive experiences.

- John Lasseter

Leadership is absolutely about inspiring action, but it is also about guarding against mis-action.

- Simon Sinek

The main tenet of design thinking is empathy for the people you're trying to design for. Leadership is exactly the same thing - building empathy for the people that you're entrusted to help.

- David M. Kelley

I don't know what leadership is. You can't touch it. You can't feel it. It's not tangible. But I do know this: you recognize it when you see it.

- Bob Ehrlich

The leader is one who mobilizes others toward a goal shared by leaders and followers... Leaders, followers and goals make up the three equally necessary supports for leadership.

- Garry Wills

I believe that the capacity that any organization needs is for leadership to appear anywhere it is needed, when it is needed.

- **Margaret J. Wheatley**

One secret of leadership is that the mind of a leader never turns off. Leaders even when they are sightseers or spectators, are active; not passive observers.

- **James Humes**

Leadership that exploits and sacrifices young people on the altar of its goals is nothing more than raw, demonic power. Genuine leadership is found in ceaseless efforts to foster young people, to pave the way forward for them.

- **Daisaku Ikeda**

Making those around you feel invisible is the opposite of leadership.

- **Margaret Heffernan**

Ninety percent of leadership is the ability to communicate something people want.

- **Dianne Feinstein**

If we are to negotiate the coming years safely, we may need a new kind of leadership. To put it more precisely, we need the rediscovery of an ancient kind of leadership that has rarely been given the prominence it deserves. I mean the leader as teacher.

- **Jonathan Sacks**

One of the sad truths about leadership is that, the higher up the ladder you travel, the less you know.

- **Margaret Heffernan**

I think leadership is knowing what you want to achieve and then purposefully and sensibly taking steps to achieve it, remembering always that you have got to bring people with you if you are seeking to be a successful political leader.

- **Tony Abbott**

For good or ill, I'm a person of leadership. I do my best. I don't dodge responsibility.

- **Gerry Adams**

One simple way to keep organizations from becoming cancerous might be to rotate all jobs on a regular, frequent and mandatory basis, including the leadership positions.

- **Robert Shea**

At the heart of great leadership is a curious mind, heart, and spirit.

- Chip Conley

Being a CEO still means sitting across the table from big institutional investors and showing your leadership and having them believe in you.

- Christie Hefner

I've never worried about payback. People are hungry for leadership that's not afraid of political consequence.

Wendy Davis

I fell in love with the topic of leadership. For three decades, that has been a major focus of my hands-on work: listening to and working with leaders, their teams and their organizations.

- Henry Cloud

I'm all for ambition and stretch goals. I set them for myself. But leadership isn't the same as cheerleading. Believing in something is a necessary but absolutely insufficient condition for making it come true.

- Margaret Heffernan

If you can provide the funding and you get the leadership, you'll have a competitive team.

- T. Boone Pickens

I think our leadership team is a highly accountable leadership team.

- Steve Ballmer

And I'd say one of the great lessons I've learned over the past couple of decades, from a management perspective, is that really when you come down to it, it really is all about people and all about leadership.

- Steve Case

I believe it is time for new leadership that is able to leave the '70s behind.

- Kim Campbell

This is easy to say with the benefit of hindsight, but I think it once again points out how very important style of leadership, that is the way he does what he does, is to his perception.

- Robert Teeter

In this nation, leadership is dollars.

- **Norman Lear**

You were born to lead as mothers and fathers, because nowhere is righteous leadership more crucial than in the family.

- **Sheri L. Dew**

Leadership is the key to 99 percent of all successful efforts.

- **Erskine Bowles**

In politics, as in business, leadership is crucial.

- **Edgar Bronfman, Sr.**

The way I would measure leadership is this: of the people that are working with me, how many wake up in the morning thinking that the company is theirs?

- **David M. Kelley**

In any leadership position, you're always going to be disappointing somebody.

- **Biz Stone**

I think leadership is more than just being able to cross the t's and dot the i's. It's about character and integrity and work ethic.

- Steve Largent

I think it is important for people who are given leadership roles to assume that role immediately.

- Bob Iger

Each year I host a leadership summit in my district, and my biggest advice to young people is get experience. Get your foot in the door.

- Aaron Schock

I would assert that highly effective leaders are made more than they're born. Every leader I know who's been highly effective has worked hard at it, and they've been students of it. The more you're a student of leadership, the more you figure out what works for you and the more effective you're going to be.

- Douglas Conant

That is what leadership is all about: staking your ground ahead of where opinion is and convincing people, not simply following the popular opinion of the moment.

- Doris Kearns Goodwin

I was brought up in a family of leaders, and I think leadership is a life sentence. I like changing things that will shape the future.

- **Jenny Shipley**

We expect our leaders to be godlike. But I feel that when people try to sanctify leadership, it puts it out of the realm of regular people. And that's where the greatest leaders come from - from the people.

- **Katori Hall**

Research shows that girls look at leadership differently than boys.

- **Anna Maria Chavez**

I think the job of leadership is to expand what can be talked about and to get consensus on the nature of the problem, and that is most of the job. Because once you do that, once you have diagnosis, treatment options are obvious.

- **Jim Cooper**

At IBM, if we kept our same leadership for 36 years, we'd be bankrupt.

- **Scott Howell**

Life isn't easy, and leadership is harder still.

- Walter Russell Mead

Leadership is happening, but it's not coming from the leaders of the old institutions. Everywhere you look, you see these extraordinary, sparkling new initiatives that are under way.

- Don Tapscott

Leadership is one of the things I really strive to excel in, in my life.

- Nate Parker

A CEO's job is leadership, problem solving, and team building. I've done that my whole career.

- Bruce Rauner

Twenty-eight years in business and you understand the importance of problem solving and the importance of efficiency, because if you don't become efficient, you don't run a business well, and you are out of business. And I think some of those principles could be applied to leadership in Washington.

- Steve Daines

Our emerging workforce is not interested in command-and-control leadership. They don't want to do things because I said so; they want to do things because they want to do them.

- **Irene Rosenfeld**

People look for their leadership to lead.

- **Mick Cornett**

Leadership is one of sports' intangibles. Guys can score, guys can fight, guys can skate faster than anybody else. But not everybody can say, 'Follow me.'

- **Paul Coffey**

I grew up in a household that revered building businesses. It wasn't thinking about leadership; it was more about building something. To build something, you ultimately have to lead.

- **Penny Pritzker**

Good leadership is to know when to go, and you only succeed as a good leader if you've transported someone else in and the company gets stronger. Then you've succeeded as leader.

- **Tony Fernandes**

I learned long ago on the battlefields of Vietnam that in a crisis, there is no substitute for clear-eyed leadership.

- Jim Webb

I'd like to believe that achieving a leadership position is all about competency, capability and ambition, so I try not to distinguish between the sexes when it comes to giving career advice.

- Heather Bresch

As much as you don't like disciplining your kids, you have to sometimes. Kids want that structure, that leadership, that guidance. I think that's what I try to give my children.

- Mark Teixeira

In today's world, leaders need only be experts in leading. Everything else can be outsourced.

- Robert Jamgotchian

<u>Work</u>

All life demands struggle. Those who have everything given to them become lazy, selfish, and insensitive to the real values of life. The very striving and hard work that we so constantly try to avoid is the major building block in the person we are today.

- Pope Paul VI

Individual commitment to a group effort - that is what makes a team work, a company work, a society work, a civilization work.

- Vince Lombardi

Choose a job you love, and you will never have to work a day in your life.

- Confucius

Opportunity is missed by most people because it is dressed in overalls and looks like work.

- Thomas A. Edison

Everyone has been made for some particular work, and the desire for that work has been put in every heart.

- Rumi

It's like Forrest Gump said, 'Life is like a box of chocolates.' Your career is like a box of chocolates - you never know what you're going to get. But everything you get is going to teach you something along the way and make you the person you are today. That's the exciting part - it's an adventure in itself.

- Nick Carter

The best preparation for good work tomorrow is to do good work today.

- Elbert Hubbard

The power of one, if fearless and focused, is formidable, but the power of many working together is better.

- Gloria Macapagal Arroyo

Once you start a working on something, don't be afraid of failure and don't abandon it. People who work sincerely are the happiest.

- Chanakya

There is no substitute for hard work.

- Thomas A. Edison

The only place success comes before work is in the dictionary.

- Vince Lombardi

Working hard and working smart sometimes can be two different things.

- Byron Dorgan

Hard work spotlights the character of people: some turn up their sleeves, some turn up their noses, and some don't turn up at all.

- Sam Ewing

Far and away the best prize that life has to offer is the chance to work hard at work worth doing.

- Theodore Roosevelt

The brain is a wonderful organ; it starts working the moment you get up in the morning and does not stop until you get into the office.

- Robert Frost

Nothing will work unless you do.

- Maya Angelou

Before you start some work, always ask yourself three questions - Why am I doing it, What the results might be and Will I be successful. Only when you think deeply and find satisfactory answers to these questions, go ahead.

- Chanakya

Opportunities are usually disguised as hard work, so most people don't recognize them.

- Ann Landers

When you form a team, why do you try to form a team? Because teamwork builds trust and trust builds speed.

- Russel Honore

Nothing ever comes to one, that is worth having, except as a result of hard work.

- Booker T. Washington

Laziness may appear attractive, but work gives satisfaction.

- Anne Frank

People who work together will win, whether it be against complex football defenses, or the problems of modern society.

- Vince Lombardi

Every noble work is at first impossible.

- Thomas Carlyle

Let the beauty of what you love be what you do.

- Rumi

It is the working man who is the happy man. It is the idle man who is the miserable man.

- Benjamin Franklin

Instead of being critical of people in authority over you and envious of their position, be happy you're not responsible for everything they have to do. Instead of piling on complaints, thank them for what they do. Overwhelm them with encouragement and appreciation!

- Joyce Meyer

The only thing that overcomes hard luck is hard work.

- Harry Golden

There is joy in work. There is no happiness except in the realization that we have accomplished something.

- Henry Ford

Let us realize that: the privilege to work is a gift, the power to work is a blessing, the love of work is success!

- David O. McKay

To find out what one is fitted to do, and to secure an opportunity to do it, is the key to happiness.

- John Dewey

I've learned from experience that if you work harder at it, and apply more energy and time to it, and more consistency, you get a better result. It comes from the work.

- Louis C. K.

To find joy in work is to discover the fountain of youth.

- Pearl S. Buck

The supreme accomplishment is to blur the line between work and play.

- Arnold J. Toynbee

Luck? I don't know anything about luck. I've never banked on it and I'm afraid of people who do. Luck to me is something else: Hard work - and realizing what is opportunity and what isn't.

- Lucille Ball

Every man loves what he is good at.

- Thomas Shadwell

Working hard is very important. You're not going to get anywhere without working extremely hard.

- George Lucas

Work is love made visible. And if you cannot work with love but only with distaste, it is better that you should leave your work and sit at the gate of the temple and take alms of those who work with joy.

- Khalil Gibran

All labor that uplifts humanity has dignity and importance and should be undertaken with painstaking excellence.

- Martin Luther King, Jr.

By working faithfully eight hours a day you may eventually get to be boss and work twelve hours a day.

- Robert Frost

Quality is pride of workmanship.

- W. Edwards Deming

Every man's work, whether it be literature, or music or pictures or architecture or anything else, is always a portrait of himself.

- Samuel Butler

To fulfill a dream, to be allowed to sweat over lonely labor, to be given a chance to create, is the meat and potatoes of life. The money is the gravy.

- Bette Davis

Whatever your life's work is, do it well. A man should do his job so well that the living, the dead, and the unborn could do it no better.

- Martin Luther King, Jr.

We work to become, not to acquire.

- Elbert Hubbard

And where I excel is ridiculous, sickening, work ethic. You know, while the other guy's sleeping? I'm working.

- **Will Smith**

Every man's work, whether it be literature, or music or pictures or architecture or anything else, is always a portrait of himself.

- **Samuel Butler**

Do not hire a man who does your work for money, but him who does it for love of it.

- **Henry David Thoreau**

Luck is a dividend of sweat. The more you sweat, the luckier you get.

- **Ray Kroc**

Work isn't to make money; you work to justify life.

- **Marc Chagall**

The biggest job we have is to teach a newly hired employee how to fail intelligently. We have to train him to experiment over and over and to keep on trying and failing until he learns what will work.

- **Charles Kettering**

All things are difficult before they are easy.

- Thomas Fuller

Big jobs usually go to the men who prove their ability to outgrow small ones.

- Theodore Roosevelt

Concentrate on your job and you will forget your other troubles.

- William Feather

All wealth is the product of labor.

- John Locke

Organizing is what you do before you do something, so that when you do it, it is not all mixed up.

- A. A. Milne

Good things happen to those who hustle.

- Chuck Noll

You know, I think the greatest gift in the world is a good employee, you know, or people who can do your work for you and do it well the way you'd like to have it done. And I've always been able to surround myself with really good people.

- **Kenny Rogers**

Anyone who can walk to the welfare office can walk to work.

- **Al Capp**

The only way to enjoy anything in this life is to earn it first.

- **Ginger Rogers**

I think the person who takes a job in order to live - that is to say, for the money - has turned himself into a slave.

- **Joseph Campbell**

I believe in stopping work and eating lunch.

- **L'Wren Scott**

Life grants nothing to us mortals without hard work.

- **Horace**

Honor lies in honest toil.

> **- Grover Cleveland**

When more and more people are thrown out of work, unemployment results.

> **- Calvin Coolidge**

Can anything be sadder than work left unfinished? Yes, work never begun.

> **- Christina Rossetti**

Work, look for peace and calm in work: you will find it nowhere else.

> **- Dmitri Mendeleev**

The harder I work, the luckier I get.

> **- Samuel Goldwyn**

Work is accomplished by those employees who have not yet reached their level of incompetence.

> **- Laurence J. Peter**

If you don't want to work you have to work to earn enough money so that you won't have to work.

- Ogden Nash

Work is not man's punishment. It is his reward and his strength and his pleasure.

- George Sand

Find a job you like and you add five days to every week.

- H. Jackson Brown, Jr.

The more I want to get something done, the less I call it work.

- Richard Bach

When a work lifts your spirits and inspires bold and noble thoughts in you, do not look for any other standard to judge by: the work is good, the product of a master craftsman.

- Jean de la Bruyere

Going to work for a large company is like getting on a train. Are you going sixty miles an hour or is the train going sixty miles an hour and you're just sitting still?

- J. Paul Getty

Don't stay in bed, unless you can make money in bed.

- George Burns

The greatest teacher I know is the job itself.

- James Cash Penney

Be regular and orderly in your life, so that you may be violent and original in your work.

- Gustave Flaubert

Without labor nothing prospers.

- Sophocles

Because I have work to care about, it is possible that I may be less difficult to get along with than other women when the double chins start to form.

- Gloria Steinem

If you put all your strength and faith and vigor into a job and try to do the best you can, the money will come.

- Lawrence Welk

Give yourself something to work toward - constantly.

- Mary Kay Ash

You're blessed if you have the strength to work.

- Mahalia Jackson

When your work speaks for itself, don't interrupt.

- Henry J. Kaiser

No fine work can be done without concentration and self-sacrifice and toil and doubt.

- Max Beerbohm

Teaching was the hardest work I had ever done, and it remains the hardest work I have done to date.

- Ann Richards

I think about my work every minute of the day.

- Jeff Koons

The harder you work... and visualize something, the luckier you get.

- Seal

Without work, all life goes rotten. But when work is soulless, life stifles and dies.

- Albert Camus

My experience has been that work is almost the best way to pull oneself out of the depths.

- **Eleanor Roosevelt**

Nobody ever drowned in his own sweat.

- **Ann Landers**

Work will win when wishy-washy wishing won't.

- **Thomas S. Monson**

Work is a necessity for man. Man invented the alarm clock.

- **Pablo Picasso**

One man's wage increase is another man's price increase.

- **Harold Wilson**

One thing I never want to be accused of is not working.

- **Don Shula**

I never did a day's work in my life. It was all fun.

- **Thomas A. Edison**

It is your work in life that is the ultimate seduction.

- Pablo Picasso

Nothing is work unless you'd rather be doing something else.

- George Halas

No one can arrive from being talented alone, work transforms talent into genius.

- Anna Pavlova

Be open to the amazing changes which are occurring in the field that interest you.

- Leigh Steinberg

Labor gives birth to ideas.

- Jim Rohn

I can't imagine anything more worthwhile than doing what I most love. And they pay me for it.

- Edgar Winter

Big pay and little responsibility are circumstances seldom found together.

- **Napoleon Hill**

When a man tells you that he got rich through hard work, ask him: 'Whose?'

- **Don Marquis**

By the work one knows the workman.

- **Jean de La Fontaine**

Work is much more fun than fun.

- **Noel Coward**

I've got a woman's ability to stick to a job and get on with it when everyone else walks off and leaves it.

- **Margaret Thatcher**

The idea of having a steady job is appealing.

- **Robin Williams**

Blessed is he who has found his work; let him ask no other blessedness.

- **Thomas Carlyle**

And to get real work experience, you need a job, and most jobs will require you to have had either real work experience or a graduate degree.

- Donald Norman

Ya gots to work with what you gots to work with.

- Stevie Wonder

And if small businesspeople say they made it on their own, all they are saying is that nobody else worked seven days a week in their place. Nobody showed up in their place to open the door at five in the morning. Nobody did their thinking, and worrying, and sweating for them.

- Paul Ryan

Work expands so as to fill the time available for its completion.

- C. Northcote Parkinson

Men for the sake of getting a living forget to live.

- Margaret Fuller

It is only when I am doing my work that I feel truly alive.

- Federico Fellini

Unemployment is capitalism's way of getting you to plant a garden.

- **Orson Scott Card**

Work hard for what you want because it won't come to you without a fight. You have to be strong and courageous and know that you can do anything you put your mind to. If somebody puts you down or criticizes you, just keep on believing in yourself and turn it into something positive.

- **Leah LaBelle**

The price of success is hard work, dedication to the job at hand, and the determination that whether we win or lose, we have applied the best of ourselves to the task at hand.

- **Vince Lombardi**

A dream doesn't become reality through magic; it takes sweat, determination and hard work.

- **Colin Powell**

There are no secrets to success. It is the result of preparation, hard work, and learning from failure.

- **Colin Powell**

If you always put limit on everything you do, physical or anything else. It will spread into your work and into your life. There are no limits. There are only plateaus, and you must not stay there, you must go beyond them.

- Bruce Lee

When love and skill work together, expect a masterpiece.

- John Ruskin

A day of worry is more exhausting than a week of work.

- John Lubbock

Keep your dreams alive. Understand to achieve anything requires faith and belief in yourself, vision, hard work, determination, and dedication. Remember all things are possible for those who believe.

- Gail Devers

To be a champion, I think you have to see the big picture. It's not about winning and losing; it's about every day hard work and about thriving on a challenge. It's about embracing the pain that you'll experience at the end of a race and not being afraid. I think people think too hard and get afraid of a certain challenge.

- Summer Sanders

I have not failed. I've just found 10,000 ways that won't work.

— **Thomas A. Edison**

Look at the sky. We are not alone. The whole universe is friendly to us and conspires only to give the best to those who dream and work.

— **A. P. J. Abdul Kalam**

Without hard work, nothing grows but weeds.

— **Gordon B. Hinckley**

Follow your passion, be prepared to work hard and sacrifice, and, above all, don't let anyone limit your dreams.

— **Donovan Bailey**

Success is the result of perfection, hard work, learning from failure, loyalty, and persistence.

— **Colin Powell**

We are all born ignorant, but one must work hard to remain stupid.

— **Benjamin Franklin**

Perseverance is the hard work you do after you get tired of doing the hard work you already did.

- **Newt Gingrich**

That's been one of my mantras - focus and simplicity. Simple can be harder than complex: You have to work hard to get your thinking clean to make it simple. But it's worth it in the end because once you get there, you can move mountains.

- **Steve Jobs**

Thinking is the hardest work there is, which is probably the reason why so few engage in it.

- **Henry Ford**

We are at our very best, and we are happiest, when we are fully engaged in work we enjoy on the journey toward the goal we've established for ourselves. It gives meaning to our time off and comfort to our sleep. It makes everything else in life so wonderful, so worthwhile.

- **Earl Nightingale**

If I don't feel confident about my body, I'm not going to sit at home and feel sorry for myself and not do something about it. It's all about taking action and not being lazy. So you do the work, whether it's fitness or whatever. It's about getting up, motivating yourself and just doing it.

- Kim Kardashian

Concentrate all your thoughts upon the work at hand. The sun's rays do not burn until brought to a focus.

- Alexander Graham Bell

At the end of the day, you are solely responsible for your success and your failure. And the sooner you realize that, you accept that, and integrate that into your work ethic, you will start being successful. As long as you blame others for the reason you aren't where you want to be, you will always be a failure.

- Erin Cummings

You have to fight to reach your dream. You have to sacrifice and work hard for it.

- Lionel Messi

Focused, hard work is the real key to success. Keep your eyes on the goal, and just keep taking the next step towards completing it. If you aren't sure which way to do something, do it both ways and see which works better.

- John Carmack

Football is like life - it requires perseverance, self-denial, hard work, sacrifice, dedication and respect for authority.

- Vince Lombardi

Happiness does not come from doing easy work but from the afterglow of satisfaction that comes after the achievement of a difficult task that demanded our best.

- Theodore Isaac Rubin

Do not wait; the time will never be 'just right.' Start where you stand, and work with whatever tools you may have at your command, and better tools will be found as you go along.

- George Herbert

Through hard work, perseverance and a faith in God, you can live your dreams.

- Benjamin Carson

Inspiration is one thing and you can't control it, but hard work is what keeps the ship moving. Good luck means, work hard. Keep up the good work.

- Kevin Eubanks

The three great essentials to achieve anything worthwhile are: Hard work, Stick-to-itiveness, and Common sense.

- Thomas A. Edison

If you really believe in what you're doing, work hard, take nothing personally and if something blocks one route, find another. Never give up.

- Laurie Notaro

Work hard, be kind, and amazing things will happen.

- Conan O'Brien

Talent is cheaper than table salt. What separates the talented individual from the successful one is a lot of hard work.

- Stephen King

Winners embrace hard work. They love the discipline of it, the trade-off they're making to win. Losers, on the other hand, see it as punishment. And that's the difference.

- Lou Holtz

Pleasure in the job puts perfection in the work.

- Aristotle

Work hard. And have patience. Because no matter who you are, you're going to get hurt in your career and you have to be patient to get through the injuries.

- Randy Johnson

Follow your dreams, work hard, practice and persevere. Make sure you eat a variety of foods, get plenty of exercise and maintain a healthy lifestyle.

- Sasha Cohen

People who make the choice to study, work hard or do whatever they endeavor is to give it the max on themselves to reach to the top level. And you have the people who get envy and jealous, yet are not willing to put that work in, and they want to get the same praise.

- Evander Holyfield

I think the best way to get a good night sleep is to work hard throughout the day. If you work hard and, of course, work out.

- William H. McRaven

I love it when people doubt me. It makes me work harder to prove them wrong.

- Derek Jeter

Believe in yourself, and the rest will fall into place. Have faith in your own abilities, work hard, and there is nothing you cannot accomplish.

- Brad Henry

Dreams can become a reality when we possess a vision that is characterized by the willingness to work hard, a desire for excellence, and a belief in our right and our responsibility to be equal members of society.

- Janet Jackson

I hope the millions of people I've touched have the optimism and desire to share their goals and hard work and persevere with a positive attitude.

- Michael Jordan

I have never in my life found myself in a situation where I've stopped work and said, 'Thank God it's Friday.' But weekends are special even if your schedule is all over the place. Something tells you the weekend has arrived and you can indulge yourself a bit.

- Helen Mirren

One machine can do the work of fifty ordinary men. No machine can do the work of one extraordinary man.

- Elbert Hubbard

Confidence and empowerment are cousins in my opinion. Empowerment comes from within and typically it's stemmed and fostered by self-assurance. To feel empowered is to feel free and that's when people do their best work. You can't fake confidence or empowerment.

- Amy Jo Martin

I think it's important to always keep professional and surround yourself with good people, work hard, and be nice to everyone.

- Caroline Winberg

An organization, no matter how well designed, is only as good as the people who live and work in it.

- Dee Hock

It's all about quality of life and finding a happy balance between work and friends and family.

- **Philip Green**

Work out your own salvation. Do not depend on others.

- **Buddha**

Your ego can become an obstacle to your work. If you start believing in your greatness, it is the death of your creativity.

- **Marina Abramovic**

If you're not willing to work hard, let someone else do it. I'd rather be with someone who does a horrible job, but gives 110% than with someone who does a good job and gives 60%.

- **Will Smith**

There is a saying that every nice piece of work needs the right person in the right place at the right time.

- **Benoit Mandelbrot**

Some people see things that are and ask, Why? Some people dream of things that never were and ask, Why not? Some people have to go to work and don't have time for all that.

- George Carlin

Work hard, stay positive, and get up early. It's the best part of the day.

- George Allen, Sr.

Together with a culture of work, there must be a culture of leisure as gratification. To put it another way: people who work must take the time to relax, to be with their families, to enjoy themselves, read, listen to music, play a sport.

- Pope Francis

My grandfather once told me that there were two kinds of people: those who do the work and those who take the credit. He told me to try to be in the first group; there was much less competition.

- Indira Gandhi

All growth depends upon activity. There is no development physically or intellectually without effort, and effort means work.

- Calvin Coolidge

It was the labor movement that helped secure so much of what we take for granted today. The 40-hour work week, the minimum wage, family leave, health insurance, Social Security, Medicare, retirement plans. The cornerstones of the middle-class security all bear the union label.

- Barack Obama

The expectations of life depend upon diligence; the mechanic that would perfect his work must first sharpen his tools.

- Confucius

Pray as though everything depended on God. Work as though everything depended on you.

- Saint Augustine

In order to excel, you must be completely dedicated to your chosen sport. You must also be prepared to work hard and be willing to accept constructive criticism. Without one hundred percent dedication, you won't be able to do this.

- Willie Mays

If you work hard and you do your best, you can do anything.

- Erin Heatherton

No man ever got very high by pulling other people down. The intelligent merchant does not knock his competitors. The sensible worker does not work those who work with him. Don't knock your friends. Don't knock your enemies. Don't knock yourself.

- Alfred Lord Tennyson

There is simply no substitute for hard work when it comes to achieving success.

- Heather Bresch

The American Dream is still alive out there, and hard work will get you there. You don't necessarily need to have an Ivy League education or to have millions of dollars startup money. It can be done with an idea, hard work and determination.

- Bill Rancic

Without hard work and discipline it is difficult to be a top professional.

- Jahangir Khan

Everybody wants to be famous, but nobody wants to do the work. I live by that. You grind hard so you can play hard. At the end of the day, you put all the work in, and eventually it'll pay off. It could be in a year, it could be in 30 years. Eventually, your hard work will pay off.

— **Kevin Hart**

I learned the value of hard work by working hard.

— **Margaret Mead**

I believe that working with good people matters because then the work environment is good. If there is a sense of respect and belief among the people you work with, that is when good work is done.

— **Ranbir Kapoor**

This has always been a motto of mine: Attempt the impossible in order to improve your work.

— **Bette Davis**

Our fatigue is often caused not by work, but by worry, frustration and resentment.

— **Dale Carnegie**

Whenever you have taken up work in hand, you must see it to the finish. That is the ultimate secret of success. Never, never, never give up!

- **Dada Vaswani**

I've always believed that if you put in the work, the results will come.

- **Michael Jordan**

The reward for work well done is the opportunity to do more.

- **Jonas Salk**

I look back on my life like a good day's work, it was done and I am satisfied with it.

- **Grandma Moses**

The scientific man does not aim at an immediate result. He does not expect that his advanced ideas will be readily taken up. His work is like that of the planter - for the future. His duty is to lay the foundation for those who are to come, and point the way.

- **Nikola Tesla**

Decide what you want, decide what you are willing to exchange for it. Establish your priorities and go to work.

- H. L. Hunt

Nobody in life gets exactly what they thought they were going to get. But if you work really hard and you're kind, amazing things will happen.

- Conan O'Brien

People might not get all they work for in this world, but they must certainly work for all they get.

- Frederick Douglass

The beginning is the most important part of the work.

- Plato

All successful people men and women are big dreamers. They imagine what their future could be, ideal in every respect, and then they work every day toward their distant vision, that goal or purpose.

- Brian Tracy

I do not know anyone who has got to the top without hard work. That is the recipe. It will not always get you to the top, but should get you pretty near.

- **Margaret Thatcher**

Rest when you're weary. Refresh and renew yourself, your body, your mind, your spirit. Then get back to work.

- **Ralph Marston**

A career path is rarely a path at all. A more interesting life is usual a more crooked, winding path of missteps, luck and vigorous work. It is almost always a clumsy balance between the things you try to make happen and the things that happen to you.

- **Tom Freston**

Most people work just hard enough not to get fired and get paid just enough money not to quit.

- **George Carlin**

The average person puts only 25% of his energy and ability into his work. The world takes off its hat to those who put in more than 50% of their capacity, and stands on its head for those few and far between souls who devote 100%.

- **Andrew Carnegie**

How do you go from where you are to where you wanna be? And I think you have to have an enthusiasm for life. You have to have a dream, a goal. And you have to be willing to work for it.

- **Jim Valvano**

If you go to work on your goals, your goals will go to work on you. If you go to work on your plan, your plan will go to work on you. Whatever good things we build end up building us.

- **Jim Rohn**

Thunder is good, thunder is impressive; but it is lightning that does the work.

- **Mark Twain**

Photography is the simplest thing in the world, but it is incredibly complicated to make it really work.

- **Martin Parr**

God gives talent. Work transforms talent into genius.

- **Anna Pavlova**

I'll always use the negativity as more motivation to work even harder and become even stronger.

- Tim Tebow

I have no idols. I admire work, dedication and competence.

Ayrton Senna

Don't worry about being a star, worry about doing good work, and all that will come to you.

- Ice Cube

When you have a dream that you can't let go of, trust your instincts and pursue it. But remember: Real dreams take work, They take patience, and sometimes they require you to dig down very deep. Be sure you're willing to do that.

- Harvey Mackay

Don't do anything by half. If you love someone, love them with all your soul. When you go to work, work your ass off. When you hate someone, hate them until it hurts.

- Henry Rollins

Always continue the climb. It is possible for you to do whatever you choose, if you first get to know who you are and are willing to work with a power that is greater than ourselves to do it.

- Ella Wheeler Wilcox

Research indicates that employees have three prime needs: Interesting work, recognition for doing a good job, and being let in on things that are going on in the company.

- Zig Ziglar

Work like you don't need the money. Love like you've never been hurt. Dance like nobody's watching.

- Satchel Paige

It was my father who taught us that an immigrant must work twice as hard as anybody else, that he must never give up.

- Zinedine Zidane

If you watch a game, it's fun. If you play it, it's recreation. If you work at it, it's golf.

- Bob Hope

Work gives you meaning and purpose and life is empty without it.

- Stephen Hawking

I have a motto: Work to become, not to acquire.

- Alan Kulwicki

The highest reward that God gives us for good work is the ability to do better work.

- Elbert Hubbard

Love and work... work and love, that's all there is.

- Sigmund Freud

Employees who report receiving recognition and praise within the last seven days show increased productivity, get higher scores from customers, and have better safety records. They're just more engaged at work.

- Tom Rath

Do your work with your whole heart, and you will succeed - there's so little competition.

- Elbert Hubbard

Never permit a dichotomy to rule your life, a dichotomy in which you hate what you do so you can have pleasure in your spare time. Look for a situation in which your work will give you as much happiness as your spare time.

- Pablo Picasso

Labor wants pride and joy in doing good work, a sense of making or doing something beautiful or useful - to be treated with dignity and respect as brother and sister.

- Thorstein Veblen

You see, God helps only people who work hard. That principle is very clear.

- A. P. J. Abdul Kalam

My work is a game, a very serious game.

- M. C. Escher

Follow your dreams. If you have a goal, and you want to achieve it, then work hard and do everything you can to get there, and one day it will come true.

- Lindsey Vonn

If you work just for money, you'll never make it, but if you love what you're doing and you always put the customer first, success will be yours.

- Ray Kroc

A little less complaint and whining, and a little more dogged work and manly striving, would do us more credit than a thousand civil rights bills.

- W. E. B. Du Bois

I've got a theory that if you give 100% all of the time, somehow things will work out in the end.

- Larry Bird

Luck is great, but most of life is hard work.

- Iain Duncan Smith

The artist is nothing without the gift, but the gift is nothing without work.

- Emile Zola

The best preparation for tomorrow is to do today's work superbly well.

- William Osler

The fruit of your own hard work is the sweetest.

- Deepika Padukone

Tell the truth, work hard, and come to dinner on time.

- Gerald R. Ford

Hard work opens doors and shows the world that you are serious about being one of those rare - and special - human beings who use the fullness of their talents to do their very best.

- Robin S. Sharma

Great work is done by people who are not afraid to be great.

- Fernando Flores

When you discover your mission, you will feel its demand. It will fill you with enthusiasm and a burning desire to get to work on it.

- W. Clement Stone

Creativity is a habit, and the best creativity is the result of good work habits.

- Twyla Tharp

Strength of character may be learned at work, but beauty of character is learned at home.

- Henry Drummond

It's always such a joy that you wake up in the morning and there's work to do.

- Jerome Lawrence

I never did anything by accident, nor did any of my inventions come by accident; they came by work.

- Thomas A. Edison

Don't ever, ever, believe anyone who tells you that you can just get by, by doing the easiest thing possible. Because there's always somebody behind you who really wants to do what you're doing. And they're going to work harder than you if you're not working hard.

- Maria Bartiromo

Confidence comes from hours and days and weeks and years of constant work and dedication.

- Roger Staubach

Tell the truth, work hard, and come to dinner on time.

- Gerald R. Ford

I do not believe in excuses. I believe in hard work as the prime solvent of life's problems.

- James Cash Penney

Work while you work, play while you play - this is a basic rule of repressive self-discipline.

- Theodor Adorno

It's always such a joy that you wake up in the morning and there's work to do.

- Jerome Lawrence

There is no substitute for hard work, 23 or 24 hours a day. And there is no substitute for patience and acceptance.

- Cesar Chavez

Colleagues are a wonderful thing - but mentors, that's where the real work gets done.

- Junot Diaz

Hard work pays off - hard work beats talent any day, but if you're talented and work hard, it's hard to be beat.

- Robert Griffin III

There's no lotion or potion that will make sales faster and easier for you - unless your potion is hard work.

- **Jeffrey Gitomer**

Just be yourself. Be honest, work towards a goal, and you'll achieve it.

- **Emraan Hashmi**

Self-belief and hard work will always earn you success.

- **Virat Kohli**

There is no secret to success except hard work and getting something indefinable which we call 'the breaks.' In order for a writer to succeed, I suggest three things - read and write - and wait.

- **Countee Cullen**

You only do good work when you're taking risks and pushing yourself.

- **Sally Hawkins**

If you're interested in 'balancing' work and pleasure, stop trying to balance them. Instead make your work more pleasurable.

- **Donald Trump**

Sometimes opportunities float right past your nose. Work hard, apply yourself, and be ready. When an opportunity comes you can grab it.

- Julie Andrews

Everyone's dream can come true if you just stick to it and work hard.

- Serena Williams

Most of the time you will fail, but you will also occasionally succeed. Those occasional successes make all the hard work and sacrifice worthwhile.

- Dean Kamen

Four things for success: work and pray, think and believe.

- Norman Vincent Peale

The work of the individual still remains the spark that moves mankind ahead even more than teamwork.

- Igor Sikorsky

He who seeks rest finds boredom. He who seeks work finds rest.

- Dylan Thomas

When you have a great and difficult task, something perhaps almost impossible, if you only work a little at a time, every day a little, suddenly the work will finish itself.

- Isak Dinesen

I never did anything worth doing by accident, nor did any of my inventions come by accident; they came by work.

- Plato

Nobody's a natural. You work hard to get good and then work to get better.

- Paul Coffey

Work as though you would live forever, and live as though you would die today. Go another mile!

- Og Mandino

A good idea is about ten percent and implementation and hard work, and luck is 90 percent.

- Guy Kawasaki

In the final analysis there is no other solution to man's progress but the day's honest work, the day's honest decision, the day's generous utterances, and the day's good deed.

- Clare Boothe Luce

You discover yourself through the research of your work.

- Carine Roitfeld

The fruit of your own hard work is the sweetest.

- Deepika Padukone

The highest reward that God gives us for good work is the ability to do better work.

- Elbert Hubbard

I wouldn't say anything is impossible. I think that everything is possible as long as you put your mind to it and put the work and time into it.

- Michael Phelps

Confidence doesn't come out of nowhere. It's a result of something... hours and days and weeks and years of constant work and dedication.

- Roger Staubach

The only time some people work like a horse is when the boss rides them.

— **Gabriel Heatter**

Success in its highest and noblest form calls for peace of mind and enjoyment and happiness which come only to the man who has found the work that he likes best.

— **Napoleon Hill**

When you put a lot of hard work into one goal and you achieve it, that's a really good feeling.

— **Derek Jeter**

My philosophy of life is that if we make up our mind what we are going to make of our lives, then work hard toward that goal, we never lose - somehow we win out.

— **Ronald Reagan**

Problems are only opportunities in work clothes.

— **Henry J. Kaiser**

Great work is done by people who are not afraid to be great.

— **Fernando Flores**

It takes a lot of energy to be negative. You have to work at it. But smiling is painless. I'd rather spend my energy smiling.

- Eric Davis

Your most important work is always ahead of you, never behind you.

- Stephen Covey

If you work hard and play by the rules, this country is truly open to you. You can achieve anything.

- Arnold Schwarzenegger

No great achiever - even those who made it seem easy - ever succeeded without hard work.

- Jonathan Sacks

I come from a very rough background, and I'm saying that if you work hard and dedicate yourself that you can make it, too.

- Floyd Mayweather, Jr.

If you want to achieve excellence, you can get there today. As of this second, quit doing less-than-excellent work.

- Thomas J. Watson

Transparency, honesty, kindness, good stewardship, even humor, work in businesses at all times.

- John Gerzema

Be true to your work, your word, and your friend.

- John Boyle O'Reilly

Don't work for recognition, but do work worthy of recognition.

- H. Jackson Brown, Jr.

Follow your dreams. If you have a goal, and you want to achieve it, then work hard and do everything you can to get there, and one day it will come true.

- Lindsey Vonn

If you love your work, you'll be out there every day trying to do it the best you possibly can, and pretty soon everybody around will catch the passion from you - like a fever.

- Sam Walton

Fires can't be made with dead embers, nor can enthusiasm be stirred by spiritless men. Enthusiasm in our daily work lightens effort and turns even labor into pleasant tasks.

- James A. Baldwin

At the end of the day, both men and women who become CEOs have showed tenacity and hard work to succeed in their careers. It takes not just skills but also extreme dedication and commitment. And regardless of gender, CEOs are measured by the same criteria - the growth and success of the business.

- Susan Wojcicki

The secret is to work less as individuals and more as a team. As a coach, I play not my eleven best, but my best eleven.

- Knute Rockne

The best work is not what is most difficult for you; it is what you do best.

- Jean-Paul Sartre

Anyone's life truly lived consists of work, sunshine, exercise, soap, plenty of fresh air, and a happy contented spirit.

- Lillie Langtry

Be spectacularly great at what you do. Wear your passion on your sleeve and hold your heart in the palm of your hand. And work hard. Really hard.

- Robin S. Sharma

Your expectations opens or closes the doors of your supply, If you expect grand things, and work honestly for them, they will come to you, your supply will correspond with your expectation.

- Orison Swett Marden

The path of least resistance and least trouble is a mental rut already made. It requires troublesome work to undertake the alternation of old beliefs.

- John Dewey

I learned that the only way you are going to get anywhere in life is to work hard at it. Whether you're a musician, a writer, an athlete or a businessman, there is no getting around it. If you do, you'll win - if you don't, you won't.

- Bruce Jenner

Most people sort of enjoy going to work because of the socialisation, a chance to flirt with co-workers and so on, but actually hate the job they do.

- P. J. O'Rourke

Wherever smart people work, doors are unlocked.

- **Steve Wozniak**

I don't work at being ordinary.

- **Paul McCartney**

When many work together for a goal, Great things may be accomplished. It is said a lion cub was killed By a single colony of ants.

- **Saskya Pandita**

Whatever you want to do, do with full passion and work really hard towards it. Don't look anywhere else. There will be a few distractions, but if you can be true to yourself, you will be successful for sure.

- **Virat Kohli**

My heroes are just everyday people who work hard, are honest and have integrity.

- **Jordin Sparks**

From my dad I learned to be good to people, to always be honest and straightforward. I learned hard work and perseverance.

- **Luke Bryan**

I guess we all like to be recognized not for one piece of fireworks, but for the ledger of our daily work.

— **Neil Armstrong**

It's fun to be on the edge. I think you do your best work when you take chances, when you're not safe, when you're not in the middle of the road, at least for me, anyway.

— **Danny DeVito**

I want my kids to have a good work ethic. I believe you can achieve anything if you work hard enough to get it.

— **Victoria Beckham**

The hard work definitely paid off and hard work always does.

— **Gabby Douglas**

It's hard because people always say, 'Follow your dreams,' but it's not a perfect world, and things don't always work out. But you've just got to work hard, and you can't take things for granted.

— **Stephen Colletti**

Be different, stand out, and work your butt off.

— **Reba McEntire**

Ingenuity, plus courage, plus work, equals miracles.

- **Bob Richards**

I enjoy hard work; I love setting goals and achieving them.

- **Jewel**

You are never given a wish without also being given the power to make it come true. You may have to work for it, however.

- **Richard Bach**

Everyone has a story that makes me stronger. I know that the work I do is important and I enjoy it, but it is nice to hear the feedback of what we do to inspire others.

- **Richard Simmons**

Those who cannot work with their hearts achieve but a hollow, half-hearted success that breeds bitterness all around.

- **A. P. J. Abdul Kalam**

Good luck happens to people who work hard for it. Sometimes people just fall into the honey pot, but I've consistently strived to create whatever good fortune I can get in my life - and consistently strive just as hard not to screw it up once I have it!

- Patrick Duffy

Love and work are the cornerstones of our humanness.

- Sigmund Freud

I feel like a tiger right now. There's nothing impossible if you get up and work for it.

- Michael Flatley

I just hate losing and that gives you an extra determination to work harder.

- Wayne Rooney

Derive happiness in oneself from a good day's work, from illuminating the fog that surrounds us.

- Henri Matisse

Be prepared, work hard, and hope for a little luck. Recognize that the harder you work and the better prepared you are, the more luck you might have.

- Ed Bradley

Lazy people tend not to take chances, but express themselves by tearing down other's work.

- Ann Rule

Nothing good comes in life or athletics unless a lot of hard work has preceded the effort. Only temporary success is achieved by taking short cuts.

- Roger Staubach

I think that my biggest attribute to any success that I have had is hard work. There really is no substitute for working hard.

- Maria Bartiromo

Across professions, consistency is a direct product of work ethic.

- Harsha Bhogle

The world is full of willing people; some willing to work, the rest willing to let them.

- Robert Frost

We either make ourselves miserable, or we make ourselves strong. The amount of work is the same.

- Carlos Castaneda

Loyal and efficient work in a great cause, even though it may not be immediately recognized, ultimately bears fruit.

- Jawaharlal Nehru

Call it what you will, incentives are what get people to work harder.

- Nikita Khrushchev

We are weighed down, every moment, by the conception and the sensation of Time. And there are but two means of escaping and forgetting this nightmare: pleasure and work. Pleasure consumes us. Work strengthens us. Let us choose.

- Charles Baudelaire

Great companies in the way they work, start with great leaders.

- Steve Ballmer

When you're not concerned with succeeding, you can work with complete freedom.

- Larry David

The important thing to me is that I'm not driven by people's praise and I'm not slowed down by people's criticism. I'm just trying to work at the highest level I can.

- Russell Crowe

Those people who develop the ability to continuously acquire new and better forms of knowledge that they can apply to their work and to their lives will be the movers and shakers in our society for the indefinite future.

- Brian Tracy

You need three things to win: discipline, hard work and, before everything maybe, commitment. No one will make it without those three. Sport teaches you that.

- Haile Gebrselassie

I come from a pretty working-class neighborhood in Chicago. Hard work was just expected of you. It wasn't some noble thing you did; it was a prerequisite. It's what a man did. You get up, you put on your boots, and you work hard. We've lost a lot of that, I'm afraid.

- John C. Reilly

The only method by which people can be supported is out of the effort of those who are earning their own way. We must not create a deterrent to hard work.

- **Robert Taft**

www.ingramcontent.com/pod-product-compliance
Lightning Source LLC
Chambersburg PA
CBHW070925290526
45795CB00001B/429